To the ocean and all her creatures

Let me tell you about something very special

Swimming with Dolphins

LAMBERT DAVIS

SCHOLASTIC INC.

New York Toronto London Auckland Sydney
Mexico City New Delhi Hong Kong Buenos Aires

This book was originally published in hardcover by the Blue Sky Press in 2004.

ISBN 0-439-67847-1

12 11 10 9 8 7 6 5 4 3 2 1   5 6 7 8 9 10/0

Printed in the U.S.A.   08

First Scholastic paperback printing, May 2005

that happens from time to time on our island.

Early in the morning, just after the sun rises,
my mother and I go down to the beach and wait.

We watch the ocean . . .

. . . and if we are lucky, we see dolphins.
Today there are five.

Two of them leap high into the air.

My mother and I put on masks and snorkels.
We dive into the water and swim out.

Dolphins swim toward us.
Then they are all around us.

There is a baby with his mother.

They swim side by side.

My favorite dolphin is the one I call Shorty.

I have seen her many times before.

I gently touch her smooth skin,
and she swims with me.

Together we glide.

We dive and surface.

We talk with bubbles and clicks.

We spin and turn.

We wave our tails in the air.

We swim until it's time to go home.
Then my mother and I head back to the beach.

Off they go, our dolphin friends,
to play, to fish, and to explore.

They catch one wave and then another.

They travel together down the coast.

We laugh and wave as we watch them go.

Our dolphin adventure is over, until another day.

AUTHOR'S NOTE

DOLPHINS, whales, and porpoises make up a group of marine mammals called cetaceans. Cetaceans live in the oceans and seas on our planet Earth. *Cetacean* comes from the Greek word for sea monster. But they are not sea monsters or fish, even though they have fins and live in the water. Dolphins, whales, and porpoises are all mammals just like you and me. They need air to breathe. The mothers make milk to feed their babies. They are warm-blooded. They live in family groups and care for their youngsters longer than most other animals.

There are many different kinds, or species, of dolphin. They live in all the world's oceans, most of the seas, and even some of the rivers. Some kinds live in shallow coastal areas while others prefer the vast areas in the middle of the ocean far away from land. The largest member of the dolphin family is the orca. An orca can be more than thirty feet long and weigh more than three tons. Hector's dolphin, which is four to five feet long and weighs around 100 pounds, is one of the smallest.

The dolphins in this book are common dolphins. They are one of the most plentiful and widely distributed species of dolphins. Adults can measure six to eight feet in length and weigh between 155 and 245 pounds. Common dolphins are one of the most colorful, with a yellow side patch and a crisscross or hourglass pattern, which makes them easy to identify. The markings can be slightly different depending on where they live. Common dolphins can be found in large schools of more than 1,000 animals or in smaller groups, like the one in our story. They can be very noisy, squealing or whistling. Maybe it's their way of talking to each other.

Dolphins also have a system to find food or find their way from one place to another when it is dark or the water is too murky to see. It is called *echolocation*. A dolphin sends out sound waves that bounce off objects, allowing the dolphin to sense what is around it. Whales, porpoises, and bats also use echolocation. Dolphins eat small fish and squid. Common dolphins are fast swimmers and very acrobatic. They can jump, tailslap, and even do somersaults. Common dolphins are always a joy to see.

Dolphins have inspired people for a very long time. Thousands of years ago, the ancient Greeks and Romans told stories and made artwork featuring dolphins. Common dolphins would have been very familiar to them. Over the years, there have been many stories of dolphins helping sailors, fishermen, and swimmers in trouble. One of my favorite stories is about a dolphin that saves a musician from pirates.

Dolphins continue to inspire people today. These intelligent, adaptable creatures are the star performers in marine parks around the world. For many people, marine parks provide the only opportunity to see dolphins. However, the best way to experience dolphins is in their natural environment. Simply by taking a walk along the beach, it's possible to see a pod of dolphins cruising along just beyond the breakers. You may wish to look into organized tours to increase your chances of success. Commercial dolphin-watch vessels operate out of many ports as well. Today, in a few places such as Australia, it is possible to swim with dolphins using a mask to see and a snorkel to breathe, like the people in our story. Having the guidance of a trained naturalist is essential to ensure the safety of both dolphins and humans.

Many times, dolphins seem to welcome encounters with humans, and perhaps they are as curious about us as we are about them. We can't really know what they're feeling. But as we increase our knowledge and awareness of these flipper-slapping, wave-riding, energetic acrobats, we can't help but value and appreciate the oceans and all the creatures that live in them.